The philosophy of life

By Zeyad Zeyadeh

ISBN: 978-1-956525-21-2

Preface

I've always wanted to be a teacher, not necessarily in school, but I wanted to talk about life, behaviors and share my thoughts.

Writing this book was challenging but I believe that this book will change many lives by giving away the recipe for a better life and addressing the most heated questions.

Table of contents

Preface 3

Table of contents 4

Life 9

Be a teacher 10

Depression 12

Social media and technology....................14

Friends and Family 16

Love and Hatred...18

Trust 19

Personality..20

Nationality and Politics..............................21

Perspectives and Empathy 22

Normalization 24

Power..25

Music 26

Think 28

Freedom 29

Religion 30

Racism & Loyalty..32

Unite 34

Work 9-5 or build a business 35

The bf & gf dream 37

Peace 39

Death 40

Manners 41

Happiness 42

Success 43

Equality and Feminism 45

Time 47

Accountability 48

Overt and Covert behavior 49

Silence 50

Looks 51

Healthy Lifestyle 53

Palestine 54

Conscience 56

Conflict 57

Motivation 58

Parents and children 60

Reading and writing books 62

Celebrity 63

Introvert 65

Faith 66

Jealousy 67

Zodiac signs 69

Bad habits 70

Pornography 71

Smoking and drinking 73

Animals and Nature 74

Money 75

Physiological stress 76

Failure 77

Fear 78

Molecular and Moral behavior 79

Brain 80

Ungrateful 81

Listening to people 82

Charity 83

Continuous learning 84

Cryptocurrency 85

Honesty 86

Gossip 87

Maid 88

Revenge 90

Values 91

Entertainment 92

Home 94

Humor 95

Curiosity 96

Discipline 97

Change...98

In the end..99

References..100

Life

We live in a big world that consists of sand, water and lands, wind, sun and plants.

Here, Humans and animals live together, there are also angels and jinns whom we can't see.

However, god's greatest creation is simply us humans.

Be a teacher

The profession of teaching is not as it used to be, it was truly respected by the people, government, etc. But now, even a lot of teachers are disrespecting their own job. The profession is dying and it's getting disrespected by everyone.

It needs some reviving, starting with the governments. If they want to prepare the youth for a better future, then they should start with the teacher and what they teach them in school.

Most of the subjects are whose need is not required in our daily life or in the future, or we need to learn things more than we need to learn those subjects. For example, math is good but why do one have to learn mathematics when they aren't planning to study anything that is related to it. Yes, I agree we need to learn how to calculate but that's pretty much it, I believe it's just wasted time and wasted brain cells, instead, give them financial lessons, social skills lessons and teach them things that they love and show interest in.

There are plenty more that can be more useful than just history and math, which is hated by most students, and that's why the schooling system is failing. It's because they made so many subjects boring and hated because they depend on memorizing not understanding.

The same problem is in colleges. For me, I entered and finished college, and got my bachelor's degree in accounting and I can easily confirm that college is not needed, you don't need a university to learn stuff and university, is just a waste of time.

All of this is being said governments can improve the education system and make it ten times better, which would help the country economically and socially.

Another thing is we people must give the youth advice when asked, be a teacher to them, be an example, show them the way we did things but at the end, let them choose their way because time changes and the ways of doing stuff changes too, if every single human be a teacher to someone, the Earth would be a better place.

☐

Depression

Depression, a word that many people use to describe their mental health. A wise man once said "Depression means you are tired of the character you're trying to play". Depression can be caused by things that happened in the past, happening now or going to happen in the future. As the suicide rates increasing alarmingly, everyone should know this.

Don't let your brain control you because if it does, you're in real trouble. You'll be needing help, but the sad thing is no matter how much people try to help you, you are your only savior.

I've had hard times, when I moved to a place I was not raised in, I couldn't adapt to people there, I felt alone although I had few people around me, which leads to a dark place. Being stuck between four walls was difficult, being emotionally down and only searching for negatives, I realized that I was the sole reason for that, so I didn't want anyone to know what's happening to me. I didn't want anybody to feel sorry for me. But now, looking back at it I perceived i was weak at the beginning I admit it, but now I look at things in a better light, I believe I benefited from that experience so much.

For anyone who is suffering from depression, this is my advice to you, The most important thing is to get closer to God because no one will help you like he does, no one will listen to you as he listens, you need to get some rest, get relieved from your stress, learn to live with yourself. It doesn't matter if you're alone, it can be quite beneficial for you. Loneliness will make you understand yourself better.

Be yourself, don't try to fit in, because at the end of the day the hardest thing in life is the fight between the outside you and the inside you, so just be you.

Social media and technology

Social media, or should I say show-off media, is the place where you can find all different kinds of hypocrisies. If you don't follow this celebrity or influencer, you won't be considered cool at all. Putting so much importance on likes from a picture you posted just to satisfy your own vanity or to get validation… so much here is artificial and fake that people are full of trust issues. It's an immature place to be in where you can fall into a lot of traps. You can even see someone blindly imitating a celebrity, just to get attention and benefits.

Social media has removed privacy and can ruin your social life if you're not able to control it. Also, it only shows the good side of us, the accomplishments. But it doesn't show the struggles which cause wrong perspectives.

On the other hand, it's a great way of communication, to get people closer to each other. Here, people have a voice, with which they can express their opinions, build some businesses. The downside is, it has gotten to a point where most of us don't use it wisely, if we can use the internet and social media for good purposes, we could be at the top, living life twenty years into the future.

Technology, in general, is something that became has become so valuable in our lives. You can search and find anything you want on the world wide web easily, using laptops and phones.

In other words, technology built an empire, but if not used wisely it can destroy the same empire it created. Therefore, it's a double-edged sword. Everyone these days uses social media and technology, but I believe that the least we could do is spread awareness across the world because every time we improve or solve something, it leads to another problem.

Friends and Family

One of the most valuable blessings we have in our lives is having family and friends. Always ask them how they're doing, what they are suffering from, what they have accomplished because these simple questions are very valuable and can make their day.

Learn to appreciate them, always give them hugs, eat with them, have fun with them, explore the world with them… Don't ever take them for granted, take care of them with love. And even after doing all of this to them, feel that this is not enough. That you will always be willing to do more for them.

Admit your mistakes. I lost one of my closest friends just because I wasn't able to admit my mistakes. We still talk but things between me and him can never be like before. It happened when I was irrational and young, I wasn't able to think straight and didn't care to admit my mistakes. Put your ego aside when you're with your loved ones.

Apologize if you did something that bothered them. The atmosphere between you might feel tense every now and then, but you should know that deep down they love you no matter what. Don't force them to do something they don't want to do, never talk behind their backs, which is the problem in many people's relationships.

Listen to them. What's the value of being a family member or a friend if you don't listen to them? Let them express their feelings. Expecting everything to go your way is not reasonable. Sometimes you must sacrifice your own joy for their needs.

Love and Hatred

The emotion of love and hatred, though opposite to each other, it is present in everyone. But few people only ignore one of them, and those are the people who are willing to make a change in the world in a good or a bad way.

Some people are hateful. But I believe it's too risky to hate someone because hate can poison your heart and soul, leading to self-hatred to others. Yet, there are a lot of people hating and discouraging people, just to feel good about themselves by feeling superior, the thrill of power and the ability to get away with their wrongdoings.

Even if you don't like someone or something, why must you hurt them? Why must you say something mean? Talking about people behind their backs is a sign of weakness.

If someone is hating on you, you either shield yourself or reply with love and I believe these two choices are the right thing to do. There are claims that love makes you weak and vulnerable, which I completely disagree with because when one sacrifices something for love, that means they are strong. They are not selfish.

This is a huge problem in our society because most people prefer to use hate more than love, which is wrong. It's like selfishness is the new way now. If it was up to me, I would choose to make the world full of love and joy. The more we spread love, the better the Earth would be in many ways.

Trust

Everyone must have somebody to trust. But the question is, why do we need it? What benefits do we get from it? There are many things you can benefit from trusting someone close- gaining courage and self-confidence and improving communication skills and relationships. Because let's be honest, you don't talk to the people that aren't close to you like you talk to the ones that you're close to, right? You are comfortable to talk to them about anything and they listen to you, keep your secrets and help you whenever you want.

Don't be afraid to trust someone who deserves your trust, just because of traumas that happened in the past. Give them their chance of gaining your trust, because the ones who didn't work for you, probably didn't deserve your trust.

The people who only trust themselves will suffer from stress, it isn't wrong only to trust yourself but surely, it's the harder way of going with things.

Personality

When someone talks about personality, most people believe it's about their public behavior only and judge people that aren't that good socially, thinking that they don't have a personality which is 100% wrong. Everyone has a personality. If I wanted to describe the word personality, I'd say it's a set of behaviors that someone has, such as the way one thinks, feels and behaves, which is possible partly due to genetics and mostly developed by the environment they are in.

Some people love their personality. Some people hate some parts of it which has become so common these days that they keep wishing for it to be different and try to change the totally unproblematic parts of it just because they thought it's not enough for them to fit in or they want to be like someone else. For example, a shy person or asocial might wish they were more outgoing. We can't change everything in our personalities because some things are like a cornerstone within us, but other things can be changed such as beliefs, goals and habits. These three things can impact personalities so much, but it's not necessarily easy to change them.

Personally, I have made changes to my personality in the last couple of years. I feel I need to do much more, because to be honest, even though I have made big changes, there is so much left to do. So, if I can do it, you can do it too.

Nationality and Politics

Why is everyone judged by their nationality and not by their actions? Humans should be judged by their actions, not by a piece of paper saying from where they belong. Some people treat you like you can choose your nationality, it's not like one can decide where they are born in.

Even countries actions don't help at, with all their terms and conditions, like restricting the citizens of a country from entering some specific countries. All of this is based on the country's politics. The decisions are always based on how they are doing economically, the benefits and support they are getting from us. And this results in common people being implicated and troubled. It's like politics first and foremost job is to disunite us, spread strife all over the world and manipulate information to suit their needs, and that's why, my dear friends, I hate politics. So, I'll ask it again, why do people suffer? Because of their nationality? Aren't we all humans?

Perspectives and Empathy

A perspective is the way you look at things. It can be a negative view or a positive view. It can be affected due to life experiences. For example, let's say you have a friend who he is constantly in an angry mood, all the time. You would get frustrated and try to make him understand how much it bothers you, and maybe fight with him if he crosses your limits. You'd believe that you are on the right side. He should be the one calming down and he probably should, but in his perspective, he can't help it.

Maybe something stressful is happening back at his home that is making him so angry and the outbursts are the result of it. Maybe he is having monetary problems. I am not saying that what he is doing the right thing, it is his way reliving his bad energy. What I am trying to say is, if we can put all the probabilities that might be bothering him and take it under consideration, it can help us relate to and understand him better and help us be more compassionate.

We should always try and forgive people and have some empathy. If you want to change your perspective towards your friend, you should stop complaining about their actions. You will find yourself trying to understand and analyze the situation as best as you can. This would result in you not responding to him based on the probabilities that you thought of, but instead you would be asking him if he is ok, offer him your help or sympathize to the best of your abilities.

See, everyone has their perspectives, and no one wants to be misunderstood by the person in front of them, which most of the times leads to conflict.

Every action has a reason and that's a universal rule. Have some empathy and understand that there always be two or more sides of the same story. You may see things from your perspective, but you can't walk in somebody's else shoes, you can only predict.

Normalization

Nowadays, when I hear the word normalize, I instantly know what one is going to say is going to be wrong. If I had to describe it, I'd say it's a way of saying that something is normal, which would be wrong in most cases for the public to accept it.

The goal of this word is to hypnotize us, to make us accept something abnormal or unacceptable and by using the word "normalize", they want to make it seem normal, forcing us to accept a certain thing and making us accept it the way it is. But everyone knows deep inside what the truth is, and what they are doing is wrong. They are just running away from the truth, and if a person doesn't accept it, you'll see all types of hate targeted towards them.

Most famous people are scared to say something against those normalized topics so they either don't talk about it or they agree with it, just to maintain their fame and generous appearance. No one loves people hating on them, but a frank person can speak up regarding these issues without caring that much about the meaningless things that others attach so much importance to.

Power

Power is what everyone desires. There are a lot of forms power comes in, like, coercive power, reward power, legitimate power, expert power and referent power.

Coercive power involves using the threat to make people do what they want to get done. Reward power suggests giving rewards get a person to do what the person holding power wants. Legitimate power is the power of position. The higher hierarchy, more is the power. Expert power is the power of knowledge and skills. Referent power is about having a following, which is usually the case of an influencer or a celebrity which I will come to talk about later. [1]

I believe there are still two missing forms of power people don't talk about that much that is, power to hold yourself back. It is a skill of holding yourself back when you get angry. And the other is the fake power, which is the power you get when you glorify yourself at someone's expense.

Identify what kind of power you use every day and judge whether if it's good or bad in your opinion. That way, you can eliminate the bad ones and keep the good ones.

Music

There is nothing like listening to music, at the beach, while driving your car, or even at home. It's just so relaxing, inspiring, don't you think?

So, here's the bigger picture. Some will say music is important and it lowers your depression and anxiety levels. It helps you work more effectively and all that high energy stuff. I disagree with this. I believe, music influences people a lot, but in a negative way. It causes illness, depression, and aggression which is the opposite of what researchers say.

Let's say you were driving your car back home and you had a bad day, what type of music will you open? Sad music that will show you that the world is so cruel and you are oppressed, right? In other words, it will fill the gap of emotion with fakeness just to show you how right you are right. This will lead to aggression, and even if you weren't sad and listened to them, you will feel depressed and empty. Eventually, when you close the music and feel calm again, you realize you have been torturing yourself the whole time without knowing. The same applies to every type of song.

This is caused by the lyrics and the beat. These days, the lyrics are so filthy and people love it just because of that. This makes our minds corrupted. From cursing to involving vulgar details in the lyrics, which sadly has been normalized, the public not only just accepted it, they even started using it.

The beat is just hypnotizing us, which has frequency programmed to make us listen to them more and more. This messes the judgement of people and it's all because of hertz. Every emotion has its own frequency, and with a manipulating beat, words can be more effective.

Personally, I started listening to music when I was 15, and I didn't like it that much but after a couple of years I started to listen more and more and my life started going downhill. There was a phase in my life when I was pretending to be someone I'm not, a phase full of depression and aggression, a phase where I faked happiness and sexiness. I understood the state of the artist is either good or bad based on their lyrics, and I also understood that it doesn't have to be my state too.

So, I would highly recommend lowering the time you listen to music. Not listening to it would be even better for our ears and brains.

Chaos is running through everything.

Think

The way you think as an individual is the most important thing. A lot of people nowadays don't use their brains or use them in the wrong way. God gave us an unmatched gift, and therefore, we should use our gift and most importantly, use it correctly.

There are different kinds of thinking- convergent analytical thinking, critical thinking and creative thinking. Convergent analytical thinking is the process of coming up with the best answer to the question using memory and resources and logic, and it's not that hard to apply but it's also not the best way either.

Critical thinking is analyzing something very thoroughly and breaking it up into fragments of information and making a judgment based on it. People nowadays criticize these kinds of thinkers because for them, such people are complicated and mean a lot of trouble, which is not correct! People that have critical thinking are the people that want to make a change to the world and don't follow blindly what people tell them.

Creative thinking is thinking about unusual topics, and by doing that, they generate new ideas. Some people consider it as an illogical way of thinking, but that's not the case. A creative thinker thinks many steps ahead of a normal thinker. [2]

It's good for us to identify our attributes as thinkers because by identifying, we can improve our thinking and thought process and learn new types of thinking.

Freedom

As time passes by, day after day, generation after generation, the amount of freedom is increasing across the years more and more. But the question is, should we strive for more?

I believe that we all should have the free will of doing anything we want because that's what differentiates us from any other creature God made. But ask yourself, why do holy books exist? It's a message from God, to obey his orders and not only to do what he told us not to but also, it's a way of valuing our moral behaviors.

Freedom, when used right, is a great thing but doing wrong things in the name of freedom is unacceptable. Maybe we can do something to stop this kind of activity and maybe we can't, but the truth is more freedom we get, more chaos would come with it and that's why I believe we shouldn't strive for more.

We should treat our wills carefully, judge them fairly, and with the help of the holy books, we should do what is right. Only God knows what is best for us.

Religion

All of us humans are born with different religions. We inherit our religions from our parents but I always used to ask myself, what if I am practicing the religion not meant for me? Because I believe, religion is the most important thing for us as human beings. This life is a test that everyone currently alive is taking, if I fail it, I'll be going to hell and if I succeed, I'll be going to heaven. I prefer the afterlife more than this world. I've always believed in God but I had to search for the truth, which is the suitability of the religion I'm practicing.

First of all, to any atheist out there reading this, I advise you to seek the truth. Look at the world, do you believe that everything has happened by chance? Do you believe that everything can be explained by science? Do you believe everything happening on the earth won't be judged? Do you believe that courts are enough to judge people? Because if that's the case, nothing we are doing has value, right or wrong. But that's not the case. This life has so much more meaning than this, God has a test for everyone; the harder it is, the more rewarding it will be.

So, don't be materialistic. What He wants from you is to believe in his existence. For me, that were my thoughts about this topic by the age of 20. I've always believed in God and I believe everyone should decide on their own what their religion should be.

The one you are following by virtue of your parents maybe right or wrong. So, please everyone, it's a win-win situation for you. Either you change your religion to what you believe is right for you or you gain more faith towards your religion because it's important to be convinced that your religion will show you the right path. It took me a lot of time to figure out the right path but in the end, I was happy and convinced about my current religion.

I was born a Muslim and I thank God for that gift. I gained more faith and started having a stable relationship with God. I do that by praying every day, and as a Muslim, I believe in every prophet that came to share the message and their books. I believe that prophet Mohammed, peace be upon him, is the last messenger and Quran is the last holy book which is valid for use at any particular time. I want everyone reading this book check the religion of Islam, which is the religion of peace. I can assure you it's not like what they say on TV. I can tell u that much, and as Jesus, peace be upon him, said: "know the truth and the truth will set you free". [3]

Racism & Loyalty

Racism is what everyone is fighting nowadays worldwide. Can we end racism? It is a very difficult question and to be honest, I believe not. Let me explain. I believe that racism is based on loyalty and loyalty will never end. For example, you watch sports. Let's say it's an international match. Almost everyone would be supporting their own national team. Why? Because they are loyal to their country and want to see their fellow players to win. Let's say a player does very bad in a match, what would you do as a supporter? You will be criticizing him in every way possible, why? Because you're loyal.

The same can be said for feminists. They criticize the system and say that it is advantageous for the men because they are loyal to their gender and do not get me wrong, I don't agree with most of the things they claim, which I'll come to later.

The same for black people. The n-word is a serious deal for them but they allow themselves to use it, which is the most said word by a black man or woman. They feel offended when a white man says it because they are loyal to their skin.

There are many cases like these but the idea is still the same. I believe that if we want to end racism, we have to end loyalty which I believe isn't achievable unfortunately. We can't remove loyalty from human beings but what we can do, is not just to talk about it.

Stop talking about the racism that happens in sports, stop talking about how women are not equal to men and stop restricting the use of the n-word. Just stop talking about it. This is the only way. Doing so won't end racism entirely, but it'll lower it so much for sure.

Unite

We are people from all different places on Earth. Try not to differentiate between anyone, help people. In other words, unite. Unity gives confidence, strength, happiness and peace.

The sad fact is that in every particular time frame there will be people working on dividing us, causing chaos. In such situations, we must resist and fight the chaos and injustice.

I have many dreams in life and one of them is living on earth without borders. Just people united as a nation because I believe that borders separated us. With borders, the higher ups get to control you better, and because of that, different groups has come into existence.

Work 9-5 or build a business

After finishing school and university, you head into another phase. Either you choose to work with your college degree, or you try to build a business or being forced to do both which is the case for most people who want to make a business but can't because of their financial status.

Let's start with a 9-5work. A 9-5 work is what most people head to after they finish their degree. It offers them a monthly salary, health insurance, and some of them offer school and housing allowances, all of that is in exchange of your work. You can even have an increase in salary after a promotion, which you get by hard work and experience. That's all the positive aspects it has. As for the negative ones they include working from 9-5 every day takes most of your day time and having a limited budget. You will climb the ladder but eventually, promotions will stop and you will get to the retirement age. That will end your increase in salary.

As for building a business, it's an option for only a few people because it's the way riddled with more failures than successes, but actually, failure is the core of any business. And the people who choose to do business, are the ones who follow their heart and have a purpose. Start small and grow bigger, you are your own boss. There is no particular time for work,

35

you can work whenever and wherever you want. You decide your salary. And if done well, it can grow and bring an insane number of returns, which will turn your small business into a big one.

As for the negative aspects of starting a business, they are- it has higher risk compared to a corporate job, because if the company goes bankrupt, there is no one to save you, and there is no certainty that your business would be successful.

There is no perfect job. It just depends on personal preferences and in the end, you choose what you want to do and bear the consequences, whether good or bad. All I can do is to give advice to both sides. My advice for business builders is to find a solution of a problem that exists and then you have to be patient, expect the losses in the beginning and learn from your mistakes, enjoy the process and good results shall come to you at the end.

My advice for the 9-5 job workers is not to put liabilities on yourself when you don't have a big source of income such as marriage or buying a car on debt because liabilities will make you poorer, and buying assets will make you richer. Cash flow for both options is essential.

The bf & gf dream

When you become a teenager, all you think about is having a girlfriend and how life with her must be so nice. So, you go and try to find one, and when you find the girl of your dreams, people advise you to go talk to her, send her a message or flowers to impress her. After everything is said and done, the outcome 60% of the time is the girl agrees to his proposal but accepts him as a friend for the time being. That means you are friend-zoned. 39% of the time she will close the door at you and only 1% of the time she will accept to become your girlfriend.

I realized that when the 1% of girls accept the boys' proposals, it doesn't happen out of luck. I was shocked knowing that the 99% of men treated women nice and gently, and the 1% whom the girls choose, treated them like they don't care about them at all and sometimes they are not even being nice to them. I just can't understand the logic involved. Why do girls not like someone interested in them? Almost everyone is becoming mean to get a girlfriend and this thing shocked me so much!

I came up with a conclusion that even if the man was attracted to a woman and she friend zoned him, he will still accept it in the hopes of one day she would be his girlfriend (60%) of times, and that's why the (39%) of times the girls close the door at you. It's because they know the game and are not interested to play it or fall in any traps. The same goes for girls.

This led me to realize that women and men can't have even normal friendships with each other [4], and that's why marriage is the solution. The (1%) is growing every day, they believe that it's normal to have a girlfriend and even have sex with her, but no, it's not okay if you aren't married to that woman.

Why? Because there has to be a guarantee for the rights of both parties. It's as simple as it sounds, marriage guarantees your rights materially and morally. That's without bringing the bad things sex can between a boyfriend and girlfriend, the diseases that can be spread by it, unwanted pregnancies, etc.

Having a girlfriend in my opinion, is a relationship that is based on fear of being stabbed behind the back for both parties, which is one of the most troublesome things the (1%) of people can suffer in life. And that's why almost every religion prohibits the relation between man and women without marriage. We have been told that we need a boyfriend or a girlfriend our entire life, but It's all a delusion. What we need is marriage and they made it look like it's bad thing.

Peace

Peace is so important in life. People used to admire individuals with luxuries but now, they admire people with inner peace. We need peace in heart and mind, we need peace to have a strong mental health, we need the peace that comes from joy and adventures.

When we go to the beach, we get to breathe clean, fresh air. In the same way, we need to admire the nature to be more in peace with our surroundings. Nowadays people are obsessed with perfection. They need to stop. Perfection is not a need. We need love, happiness and dreams because they are fabulous.

Unfortunately, sometimes there is no other choice other than war to get peace. Sometimes we fight with the outer world for some peace and sometimes there are internal fights that goes on inside. But however difficult it may be, do not lose hope in your pursuit of peace.

People should know that the real source of peace is God. So, appreciate the Lord, because not only does He gives us peace on Earth but also, he gives us eternal peace in the afterlife.

Death

Death is the end of everything and the start of something new. I am yet to taste the death of someone close to me, but I saw people close to me losing people close to them. And man! It's so painful to watch them being so sad, heart-broken and in pain that I can't imagine experiencing first-hand.

It makes you question everything you do in life and then you realize that nothing really matters. Only praying to God does.

This is the norm of life. We cry for the dead, but can't change what God has written. If someone dies young, don't feel it's an unfortunate, untimely death, it's useless to think so. Death has no age.

All we can do is to always remember the dead, pray for the dead, pray to God to forgive their sins and be ready ourselves. Personally, I used to think I may have to lie in my grave forever when I die before I am judged in front of God, but now I wonder if the dead has any sense of time or not.

Say, "Never will be struck except by what Allah has decreed for us and upon Allah let the believers rely" [5]

Manners

These days, people act like manners aren't important. Bad manners are the language of the cool people and good manners are left in the dark. We are competing on who can curse more, which is as ridiculous as it can get. Some people believe it to be normal and the it shows how 'real' the person is. Well, it isn't about being real at all, I can't accept doing the same mistake as everyone, I prefer to live in my own way without being pressured.

Morality is about respecting yourself and others. When you show respect to someone you know or don't know, you make them to respect you in return, which is called reciprocation. And there is no better way to do it than having a healthy communication with each other which good manners teach us.

Don't curse just to deliver your point to someone. Don't force your way upon someone who is not willing. Most people would feel better if we talk to them with good manners and respect. Try to make someone's day with politeness. Love each other.

Happiness

Happiness, what a great state to be in! Happiness has a lot of good results which can impact friends, family, people and society, but it has also few bad results which shows up in certain occasions which are usually caused by not understanding the true meaning of happiness. For example, most people believe that you have to be happy all the time to consider yourself a happy person, which isn't the case.

You don't have to be successful to be happy, you don't have to wait for things to go your way for you to be happy. You bring things that you want in your life by working. Help people, that will make you feel better about yourself. Give more than what you receive, do what you love, spend some alone me-time. Be grateful. Now, these are the little things that would make you genuinely happy.

Don't envy anyone because of their happiness and never consider what you see in social media as happiness because that's not happiness, happiness can't be bought like they show on the internet. Happiness is a choice. if anybody wants it, they can come and get it.

Success

Everyone loves success. Everyone has their own meaning of success based on their goals, but what is exactly needed to get to your success?

A wise man once said, "If you're not willing to be a novice in something, you can't become a master at it". [6]

You need to know that everyone has talent in something, they just have to find that thing. Nevertheless, in most successful stories, talent isn't essential. Working hard is. Thinking smart is. So, it isn't a must, but it helps.

When I say work hard, I mean do whatever you can. You can stress yourself with bad thoughts or you can also stress yourself for improvements to get to your success.

When setting goals, they must be big, not materialistic. Find your purpose. Dream big and start working, I'm sure you'll get there. Being imbalanced and sacrificing things in the beginning, are one of the keys that lead to success.

Don't compare yourself to others. Compare yourself with yourself. And always remember, the biggest success will be found in you. So, invest in yourself.

Every success has positives and negatives, but not every success is right thing to get. I believe we must do what's right regardless of the outcomes. Never convince yourself that you're right or take things out of context to prove that you're right even though you know you're wrong. Accept the fact, learn from it, adjust and move on.

Be careful what you wish for.

Equality and Feminism

Equality is what every feminist seeks. Their goal is to fight the inequalities that women face daily, but I expect them to be rational and use logic and act after understanding both sides' perspectives. That way, we can deliver justice to everyone.

Feminists claim the system is men-sided, that it doesn't do justice to the hard work of women just because of their gender. They also claim that men and women don't have equal opportunities and outcomes.

Men and women aren't the same. You need to understand the fact that we are different in the way we talk, act and think. As for having equal opportunities and outcomes, it's never possible. Everyone's situation is different and there are millions of circumstances that can affect opportunities and outcomes a person receives.

Most women's main interests are to have children, raise them and find stability, while most men seek for promotions and to earn as much money as possible, no matter the job.

Equality of opportunities and outcomes cannot exist unless we kill human participation and replace it with computers, which will be an abomination! It will kill creativity and destroy human beings in more ways than imaginable. So, if any women want the same thing every man seeks, they have to sacrifice something.   Hence, instead of complaining and blaming, they should work harder to get what they want.

I'm fully supportive of women's rights and I hate how a lot of men view women, as objects, which is so wrong! But I would like to speak up for men's rights too. Lately, a lot of women make false harassment claims against men. It's democracy, they say but the claims are false most of the time.

What I believe the feminists are trying to do, is wanting to be the better gender. But the fact is that there is no better gender. Every gender has its own attributes. We complement each other. Demanding to be better than the other gender makes you unjust in the first place.

How to end this battle? What is the solution? - Focusing on yourself and not what others have. Everyone has their own circumstances and if you want something, put in the work required.

Time

Time is the most valuable asset but the special part about it is, it's free. But sadly, many don't use it wisely. The sadder part is when time is gone, it never comes back. So, make use of it while you can.

Everyone thinks that they still have time. For example, young people would feel like they still have plenty of time. They can't more be wrong because one day, they'll realize that are growing old, and time is running out very quickly.

You need to discipline yourself as early in life as you can and manage your time. There is no time for anger and laziness in our lives. I believe we need to learn the skill of saying no. With it, we can manage our time better and be more in control. If anyone thinks they are behind and it's too late, I say, "Better late than never".

Accountability

Accountability is being able to take responsibility for your own actions and it requires understanding that your actions, choices and behavior have consequences.

Most people don't or rather, can't just accept the consequences of their own doings and start blaming others for it. If they don't find anyone gullible to push the blame to or maybe they can't trick their way out, they feel oppressed, which is a not even a real feeling!

One of the responsibilities that I believe people should take is to be modest in front of people by not only wearing inappropriate clothes but also, not doing inappropriate things because if not, we'll affect other people's minds negatively.

We must face the consequences, take responsibility and solve our problems instead of trying to run away from them. With accountability, we grow and without it, we fall.

Overt and Covert behavior

Overt behavior is a visible behavior of everyone such as driving a car or eating dinner etc.

Covert behavior isn't visible such as your inner thoughts and your intentions that nobody can see. [7] What isn't visible to the world is the real you, always be the real you.

Silence

Everything has outcomes, so does silence. It leads to a good outcome in most of the situations.

The fewer words you use in communicating, the more effective it is. The more silent you become, the more thought you put into what you say. The more silent you are, the wiser you become.

Learning the skill of being silent isn't easy at all. But I can promise you, it's rewarding.

Silence helps you mentally. For example, living in a noncrowded place benefits you in lots of ways, such as increasing your focus and keeps you relaxed and relieved. You get to contemplate life, your day and about future while you are surrounded by silence.

Silence helps you spiritually and religiously. It protects you from sins and purifies your heart.

Silence is the best answer to everything.

Looks

Looks play a big role in the word of hypocrisies. People who crave attention do all kinds of stuff to their looks just to be everyone's center of attention and for what? Just to look cool, to be popular by following trends and all that nonsense? What do you get from them? Nothing, right? One of the biggest reasons for people putting this much effort into their looks is to get more popular on social media platforms.

Buying expensive clothes and chains just to show-off, taking pictures with filters to make themselves feel good, girls wearing tight clothes and shorts to show off their beauty and body shape, men going to the gym to show off their 6 packs and strength, buying cars on a bank loan just to show off and brag, these all are actually meaningless!

These days, people are going broke just by trying to act rich and look good. Rich people are going broke because all they want to do is spend some more. People are putting more time into editing and writing captions for their pictures rather than working to get a better life. They are not working towards having more self-confidence and that's why they feel so insecure all the time.

If any of these people were actually smart and really had a sliver of self-confidence, they wouldn't do any of these meaningless and time-wasting things which makes them poor.

Doing something well and sharing it to spread awareness among people to do the same is fine and shouldn't be considered as hypocrisy, but what most people do is the literal definition of hypocrisy.

Hypocrisy has levels too and too much of it can lead to becoming a true hypocrite.

In the end, it's all about intentions. Sometimes, people do these things unconsciously, but if you realize it and still do it for people to see it, that's hypocrisy in its truest sense. The truth is the only thing that matters and what's worth your time is adjusting wrong concepts.

Being cool isn't about what you show to the outside, but it's about what's inside you. Your beauty is not about you look from outside, but it's about your nature. Always remember, perfection doesn't exist.

Healthy Lifestyle

Having a healthy lifestyle is essential in life, such as waking up early, getting a cold shower, eating healthy and exercising every day.

You see, you must have a routine in life. Some people might believe it's boring; doing the same thing every day. Well, I say though it isn't easy and it requires immense will power, I advise anyone that doesn't have a routine to get one for themselves and try it out. Trust me, you will feel a lot better than you did before.

Don't eat sugars. Lower your fat intake. Increase your protein intake. Don't consume more sugars than you should. Drink more water. Don't smoke cigarettes so your lungs can breathe some fresh air.

Sometimes, someone close to you forces you to eat or drink something unhealthy under the pretext of generosity. I believe, the opposite person would be more generous if he respects your choice and helps you or motivates you with what you are attempting to do.

Be strict with yourself. Trust me, you don't want your death to be nearer because of your actions. Strive for more and always remember, health is wealth.

Palestine

We're in a world where everyone follows trends, but don't be confused when it comes to Palestine. Palestine is not a trend.

The occupation started in 1948, it's 2022 now and the occupation is still alive.

People are trying to normalize the occupation as they usually do, but everyone knows deep inside what the truth is. Children are getting killed each day, the occupation is making families homeless and if they don't accept the truth, it will soon hit them in the face.

Human rights were created for the benefit of humanity but clearly in Palestine, they don't treat everybody as humans.

I feel sad about both sides' children. Palestinian children are dying every day from bombs and starvations, and Israelis' children are being brainwashed in schools, and the government gains benefit from this. The people that are sitting and watching the show without doing anything are the same people that get everything at the expense of these innocent children. And the cycle continues.

This case isn't only a Palestinian case, this can be seen everywhere. Nobody should donate money to those organizations that cause the death of thousands of children. There are many more countries that are suffering from similar things. Please, work towards saving them.

The old will die, and time will pass, but the Earth will always remember, and the young will never forget.

Conscience

Conscience is held by moral principles adapted by individuals. It helps individuals differentiate between what is right and what is wrong and guides them on how to make decisions.

Conscience can also be affected by emotions and perspectives. Its main job is to spread peace across the world.

Every day, before going to sleep, I lay down in bed and start questioning myself about everything that happened to me during the day. I analyze every situation and think about how I could've done things better.

It's so important to have a good conscience as an individual and as a part of society. In this way, you'll be truthful and trustworthy to your work, to your friends and family and the world. It prevents you from doing every wrong thing a human being can think about, such as deceiving people. This is done by making you feel the guilt which is a common mechanism of conscience.

The sad thing is some people are suffering from abuse by having a good conscience from people who don't even listen to their conscience or ignore it. That could damage the good people and create conflict inside that person which is what happens in most bullying cases. And that's why using your conscience and developing it is so important. Without it, chaos would prevail.

Conflict

A question that keeps running through my mind is, should we always avoid conflict?

I believe that avoiding it is like being in the safe zone but that doesn't mean you're always right because sometimes avoiding it can be wrong. Whether you address the thing that is causing a conflict or not, people will get offended and criticize you. So, you might as well do or say what's right.

A wise man once said "conflict delayed is conflict multiplied"

Motivation

Don't only feel motivated to do the easy things. Easy is lazy. The harder it is the hungrier you should become. Don't wait for luck to make you rich. Make your own luck.

If the place you're in is affecting you badly, you can travel elsewhere and work. Bad habits are distractions that can get you miles away from your goals. Learn new skills constantly. Every goal you set, work like a robot for them, without stopping. Every suffering you experience is there to make you stronger. Don't wait for someone else to motivate you. Depend on yourself to motivate yourself every day

When you wake up, look at the mirror and say, "Today is another day of the progress. With the process and hard work, I will eventually turn my dreams a reality and bring greatness into my life."

Give your all. Don't postpone today's work to tomorrow. Do it now. Motivate yourself to work on things that don't hurt or affect anybody negatively.

If we all wanted to do the job or work that pays more, we would be doing everything wrong. So please, don't work at the expense of people's mental health and lives. Try to understand that no matter how motivated you are, if you don't work for it, the time will pass. You will be left with wasted energy and even less time. So, start bringing your dreams to life now. Focus on the process instead of the results.

Be the dream before you achieve your dream. Life is hard but you have to be harder. So, stop making excuses and go work for it because without consistency, you'd never make it.

Parents and children

I talked about family and friends earlier, but parents and children are on a whole other level. As for the children, your mother raised you, gave you tenderness and love. No one can love you like her. And your father, he worked so much to put food on your table and always tries to fulfill all your needs just to make you happy.

You will only have one mother and one father in a single lifetime, so appreciate them. Give them attention and love. There is nothing wrong with someone who is living with their parents, it's a sign of how much they love their parents. Even if you want to be independent and live on your own, you must visit them once a month at least, if not more. That's what it takes to be a good child.

As for the parents, I know life is hard but don't let your mood affect the relation you have with your children. Smile at them. Teach them what's right and what's wrong but, don't be too harsh on them. Don't make negative comments on every action they do. Avoid putting a lot of pressure on them. Refrain from controlling them even when they have grown up.

Don't forget to watch your kids' behavior, see how they act and what they wear because trust me, you don't want to lose them to the wrong ways of the world. Teach them their religion, teach them to be responsible. Teach them how to decide on their own. Show love to them and remind them how much you love them not only by buying them things they need but also by actually saying sweet things like 'I love you' to them.

Lastly, if you truly love them, you won't become a liability for them. Considering them your responsibility is what makes you a parent.

Reading and writing books

Reading books is a great way to learn. By doing so, you'll be reading another person's mind, understanding their way of thinking, and can learn from them.

On the other hand, I believe writing books is better because this way, you'll know yourself better. Sharing your thoughts and releasing your emotions helps a lot. There is no friend as loyal as your book.

Celebrity

Celebrity, a sentient puppet for entertaining humans. They do and act what the public say and ask of them, just to get money.

You may think that you will be happy when you get the cash but, money isn't the only variable here. Being a celebrity has a lot of negative aspects to it, for the fans as well the celebrity.

There are two types of fans, the true fans that idolize their favorite celebrities, and the troll fans that throw hate at them and think it's fun.

There are also two types of celebrities- a celebrity that tries to be an example, and you can see this clearly by their actions, ethics and responsibility. And there comes the type that doesn't even care about being a role model and they are only doing it for the money and get paid to brainwash people.

Among the fans that idolize celebrities, some of them want to be like their idols. To achieve this goal, they blindly do whatever their idol does do and say whatever the idol says. Even if the idol's personality is trash, some of them like the idol because they think that they are cute, lovely and admire their successes without realizing what price they have paid for it.

The majority of celebrities are just misleading the youth with false ambitions and polluting their customs and traditions. They don't really care about their fans. The things they do are done just to appear cool and earn money. When some of the fans realize this from face-to-face encounters, they get depression and anxiety,

As for the celebrities, they suffer from the feeling of being controlled by the fans. They also suffer from the amount of hate they get just for being a celebrity. There must be times when they must be wishing to live life like a normal human being. And when they realize it's not possible, they may get depression. The feel of being choked is not a likable feeling.

With great power comes great responsibilities [8]. I believe that the concept of celebrity is being misused by both fans and celebs. Only a few celebrities try to make themselves an ideal example. They do everything rationally, stay true to their fans and try to benefit them too, and aren't a puppet in the society. They do not back away from speaking up.

I believe instead of assigning the word celebrity to anyone that has a following, it should be used to address people that really deserve it. The ones that are truly a great example, that can lead the aspirig youth, not clowns. The things people do for money are really baffling.

Introvert

An introvert is someone that loves being private and quiet and mainly focuses on their internal thoughts, rather than seeking emotions and stimulus from the outside world.

Most introverts aren't that good socially because they prefer not to talk too much in the public. Instead, they talk with people they are close to. It is a result of mistrust and hatred for hypocrisy.

Personally, hatred for hypocrisy is the main reason for my introvert nature. If I wanted to post a story, I ask myself, "Am I posting this story just for a specific person to see it?" If the answer is yes, I lose interest in posting it anymore.

If I am in the public and have something to say, I ask myself, "Why do I want to say this thing? Is it to flex? This results in me not saying it.

I like being an introvert, it's my comfort zone. Being independent and not having a life crowded with relations is wonderful for introverts. But at the same time, most introverts, including me, need to work on getting better communication skills. We should also try to lower our fear and hatred for hypocrisy, which is what I'm working on.

Faith

Faith is a state of mind connected to the heart. It's the core of energy that gives our life a meaning.

Faith has different intensities but its objective is always the same- to help you go no matter what happens because where there is faith, there exists hope.

Faith is mostly affected by self-suggestion and that self-suggestion can be right or wrong. This is what really differentiates us as humans- our choices. I think the least we can do with our judgement is to take our time when considering the facts fairly and only then making a judgement based on that.

Personally, I believe the most important entity with whom you can put your faith in is God and his prophets. The rest comes afterwards, such as yourself. The right faith acts like a ticket which can lead you to wherever you want to be in this life and in the afterlife.

Jealousy

It's an illusion created by our own minds. It can happen between friends and family, between strangers, etc.

Jealousy can lead to envy and envy unfortunately, exists. Strangers get jealous of each other because they look better than them or care too much about materialistic things that others have and they don't. They wouldn't look at other's perspectives which, leads to envy.

To solve this, try to understand other people's perspective. They might have worked super hard to get that car or buy that watch. So, focus on yourself because what you're seeing is the result of their actions.

Don't be jealous. Instead, take it as an inspiration to strive for more. As for jealousy between friends and family, it usually when they demand attention and time from you. Let's say for example my best friend is jealous whenever I go out or talk to someone for a little longer. He would feel jealous and offended. Why? Because he feels that he owns me. Little does he know he doesn't. I have my own life and I make my own decisions.

The more you become jealous, the more vulnerable you make yourself. The other person also feels uncomfortable because he doesn't want to hurt your feelings and at the same time, he doesn't want to be controlled. Hence, it's a lose-lose situation for both of the sides.

The best solution for jealousy is to know that not everything is going to go your way. There is no fruitful result in reproach. Thinking that your friend is too good for you would not help. Instead, know your self-worth and try to understand that the same way you have a life and has control over it, he has one too and he gets to choose what he wants in life, not you. Lowering your expectations from people will lower your disappointments.

Zodiac signs

Many people are using zodiac signs to understand someone's personality.

Some even make judgments based on it. Some people still believe in astrology even though we're in 2022, which is sad. All of it isn't real or true at all. There are people don't even believe in them but still use and talk about them which can also be considered as a contribution.

Astrology is all about predictions. There is nothing scientific about it. It doesn't predict the future as some may say. Astrology spreads racism and breeds disbelief within people. And that's why, it's banned in most religions.

Bad habits

We must fight against falling into bad habits. Every time we give into our temptations and fall into the circle of bad habits, our conscious mind asks us, "Are you sure you want to do that? Because you know what you're doing is wrong".

Smoking, drinking, gambling and watching pornography and so much more are available just to distract us and make us fall into the vicious circle of never-ending bad habits. One might think that it's going to make them happier but the truth is, it makes them unhappy and weak eventually notwithstanding the few initial happy moments when they were free from consequences and guilt.

These bad habits release high levels of dopamine which is why people get addicted to them. Life is about choices and probabilities. Eliminating the probability of bad or wrong things should be the case for us if we want to improve. I have some bad habits too, but every day I try to improve and eradicate them. That is what matters the most, just whole-hearted trying.

Pornography

Pornography is an abnormal phenomenon running through our society now. It has become such a popular and profitable business because we, the public supports it so much!

With sexual abuse and rape numbers increasing every day, everyone should know this. Modern society has normalized everything in social media. Companies are paying people to do these kinds of obscene acts and are even advertising them, like ads with girls wearing revealing clothes and making inappropriate positions.

The same goes for men too. They show off their six packs. Movies contribute a lot in promoting pornography too by including sex scenes in movies. These make the young population curious and intrigued which then leads them to visiting porn sites.

The social media is brainwashing us, trying to destroy what religions taught us and spread chaos. As you can see, there are a lot of people responsible for this phenomenon and they all spread the same idea in varying degrees.

Now, porn stars are getting millions of dollars and for what? For being a prostitute for the public, for them to brainwash us and enjoy such shameful fame. It's just so shameful and morally wrong. It's hard to get rid of watching them because in these videos, you see things you may never see in your real life. Even when you get married, you will find the reality is not at all like what they show in the porn videos, which affects you negatively in your sexual life.

The amount of money they spend on producing these products is insane. They make videos with illegal relations as well, trying to make people get attracted to their step-sister or step mum or showing relations between the same gender. That most insane part is making girls wear a hijab while doing these derogatory videos, and many more just like these.

The cold truth is, none of this should be in this world, but some of it got accepted and adapted by our society whose people got brainwashed. As for people who refused to accept it, they fell victim to it eventually too as people who participated in such videos or enjoyed such videos started sending and sharing photos and videos of it, so they are succeeding in a way or another by getting money from people watching these acts.

This increases the growth of such companies as they are seen as more normal and has been more in demand. People are selling their bodies to get paid and be somebody. They want you to fall prey to this loop and mess your brain by making you a supporter of porn.

Don't let it sink in. Don't feed your wants with these things. Discipline your eyes and for all those people out there that have an addiction to pornography, I know it's hard stopping what you're doing but put a stop to it for yourself. Either marry or keep yourself from having the urge to watch it. Keep trying to remove this act and never lose hope, you will succeed one day.

Smoking and drinking

When I was a teenager, I tried smoking. I was just trying to be cool, no crazy urges. But while trying to be cool, it became a habit of mine, a bad habit I must say. Now, I thank God that I'm sober from smoking for almost 1 year and yet more to come.

As we all know smoking is bad for our lungs. And once you get addicted, even if you have little to no money, you'll still try to buy cigarettes. It's just crazy how people become blind in face of addictions.

Another type of people are the ones who drink alcohol. I can't understand why people spend their money on something that makes you not be able to think straight. Getting drunk leads to doing irrational things unconsciously, and in worst cases, alcohol can lead to rape, murder and suicide.

That's why it's banned in most religions. When you ask people who do either of these things, they answer by saying that they are just having fun, or they just want to forget something bad that has happened and they do not want to face it for the moment. If you want joy, do something that doesn't endanger you. Find a hobby. Don't wish to forget something bad. Be strong and face it, don't try to run away from it like cowards.

To all the people who want to stop, I believe in you just like my family and friends believed in me, I did whatever it takes, and lost my addiction of cigarettes. It was not easy, but it wasn't impossible too.

Animals and Nature

We, humans, are destroying the Earth. There are millions of plants and animals that are now at risk of extinction, all of this is happening because of mining natural resources and cutting trees which causes changes in the natural landscape of the place, and by pollution.

Let's say a specific plant has gone extinct. It would lead to the starvation of a certain animal, which leads to its death, and so a certain food chain will be ruined causing the death of many animals, and at the end, it would affect us too because we are at the top of the food chain.

We need the world to listen and look for a change for the better, for the sake of our mother nature, for the sake of animals and for the sake of us humans because if we keep on doing this, not only plants and animals would go extinct, we will go with them too. And with the power of technology, it's possible to make a better system that avoids pollution and use of natural resources without causing the death of millions of plants and animals.

Money

Money is never a constant, it always travels to and fro. Making money doesn't come easy to everyone but the important thing is the way it is spent. Is it spent wisely?

I'll say it again. Your brain is your greatest asset. Saving money is a bad decision because inflation and taxes will eat it up, leaving you with your money having same value.

Spend less, invest more. This should be your financial motto. The more liabilities you have, the poorer you'll become. But you must educate yourself first in order to invest efficiently. A wise man said, "why would you save money when every central bank is printing money?" [9]

The thing is, most people hate taking risks. But without adding the element of risk in your financial life, you will never grow economically. People are too afraid to lose and that's the main reason why they won't win more than they have or are getting.

Making money should be only for livelihood purposes. Money doesn't bring happiness, helping people with it does and that should be something everyone would love to do.

Some people hate money because they think it changes people. But a wise man once said, "Money doesn't change people, money only exposes people by showing the world what and how they really are".

Physiological stress

What if I'm not enough, what is that person thinking about me, Am I pretty, Am I a likable person, how do I sound, does anyone really care about me….

Pressure coming from every direction, you are hurting yourself internally, slow it on yourself, you don't want to hurt yourself mistakenly.

Physiological stress can be caused by the outer world and by yourself, it causes a lot of things, such as headaches in most cases, heart and nervous diseases in emergency cases, and that without bringing out that it's one of the main reasons for suicide.

One of the things that can get someone physiological stress is forcing someone to do something he doesn't need or want to do, it won't be done well I can assure you, the same if you force someone not to do something.

Imagine being one of the contributors that made a lot of stresses for a person and sadly, that usually happens all the time.

We should help people with physiological stress, don't be a burden to them and make it worse for them than it is.

A wise man once said, "stress primarily comes from not taking action over something that you can have some control over".

Failure

Failure is the factor that decides whether you're going to make it or not. It doesn't matter if you fail, because failing is part of the process.

You got two choices in life- either you stay down or rise stronger and hungrier than you are. Love it or not that's how success works and that's how learning works.

Failure is the best teacher you can get.

Fear

Fear is the thing that controls and consumes many people's minds. It causes anxiety which leads to more fear.

Fear is produced by thoughts, imaginary in most cases which acts like a wall that prevents you from understanding. How to overcome fear you may ask; I believe facing fears is the best way we can overcome them. Sadly, most of the time, people avoid them, also understanding that fate is the decider of everything could also help.

We should understand pain is there for us to learn, not to run away from. Hence, for the best possible outcome, just accept the pain. We act as if we are the slaves while the fears that we got are our masters. That's why we should face them, to free ourselves.

Molecular and Moral behavior

Molecular behavior is the behavior that happens unconsciously without thinking. For example, breathing. Moral behavior is a behavior that we show after thinking. For example, when you see fire, you stay away from it because you don't want to harm yourself.

We learn molecular behaviors unconsciously. Moral behaviors on the other hand are taught by parents and teachers can also be developed over time using our minds.

Be careful when developing them.

Brain

Our brains got full of negatives because of the outer world and I believe it's our responsibility to filter what we consume. Every bad action or habit starts with a thought.

We can remove that thought by not looking or listening to things that might cause that thought. I know it may be hard, but our minds must be stronger than our feelings.

Ungrateful

How can u be so ungrateful when you're living a life which is far better than others?

Many are living with hunger. Poor people can't even breathe some air if they have health problems and here you're, worried about Nike dropping the new Nike's air?

Have gratitude no matter the circumstances you're currently in.

Listening to people

The skill of listening is easy to apply and very effective. It's a sign of respect when you're listening to someone speaking, which will lead to a better relationship between you and them.

It also helps you understand how an individual think, builds trust and reduces misunderstandings and conflict. Nowadays, family members and friends constantly interrupt each other rather than having patience and trying to listen to each other while speaking. They could take turns.

That's one reason why conflicts happen inside families and friends. Every good conversation starts with a good listener, and that's a certified fact.

Charity

Charity is essential in life. It's done for the public benefit. There are people living on the streets without homes. A lot of them are victims of wars, disasters, starvations and diseases, so we must give them charity to help them in their time of need.

It doesn't have to be money to be considered as a charity. You can do charity by giving away clothes, food and medicine too. Some people nowadays don't do charity under the pretext that it has become a business for some beggars, which is true and sad at the same time.

But I don't believe that's the right thing to do. Better give it to the ones that need it the most rather than not giving it to anyone. Since this world has been created, it was unequal in a lot of ways.

Some are born rich, while are born mediocrity. Our job is to help poor people in any way possible, and there are a lot of poor people that really need your charities. So, give them as much as you can, even if it was is little.

When you do charity, the most important thing about your work is your intentions. If you intended to give charity to help a poor person then it's done, and God shall give you rewards for the charity you did. If only half of the earth's population did charity, we could end global hunger, and no one would have to be poor anymore.

Continuous learning

Even though continuous learning is so important in life, nowadays the children, the youth and the elders hate learning.
But without constantly learning, your brain cells would stop being as much effective as they were when you were young. And you would be left behind.
Now, knowledge is at everyone's fingertips. You can learn basically anything you want to learn for free. I believe everyone should constantly learn and develop their skill set no matter the age. It's better than using your phone just for having fun. With great knowledge, also comes great responsibilities.

Cryptocurrency

Cryptocurrency is the digital money with market caps. Some people love the idea and invest in it, and some hate it and believe it's risky.

The truth is, it has both advantages and disadvantages. Having market caps in cryptocurrencies helps with reducing inflation, which usually happens with normal money because they have unlimited market caps. It removes intermediaries such as banks, therefore there aren't any process fees, and it can also increase in price ten times faster than stocks do.

As for the disadvantages, it is not regulated by authorities yet. You may lose your virtual wallet to scams, cyberattacks and hackers, and it can decrease in price rapidly being one of the riskiest investments you can invest in.

I believe in unity and with bitcoin, that same unity exists. I believe that cryptocurrencies will be everyone's future currency, but it still has a lot of room for improvement. The only thing that brought equality efficiently is the blockchain but still, it will bring more problems with it unfortunately.

Honesty

Honesty is being truthful to everyone about everything, but most importantly it's about being honest to yourself.

There is a story that most of us have been told about when we were young. It is about a farmer who had a lot of sheep. Every day he would lie about wolves eating all his sheep and run to the neighborhood screaming and shouting for help. When the villagers go to help, they find out that he was lying. There came a day when wolves really attacked his place, so he goes to his neighborhood shouting and asking for help, but everybody refuses to help him because they thought he was lying yet again. All of his sheep got eaten by the wolves. Lie's rope is too short so, 'Be honest'.

Gossip

Gossip is talking behind someone's back with a third party. This creates conflict between individuals and unfortunately, nowadays most people are backbiting each other. It's normal to think about different aspects of people, but it isn't polite when you talk about them behind their backs.

Even if you wanted to talk about an issue regarding them, it's not nice. When you talk about someone and they are not present there, you better talk nice about them. A wise man once said, "Small minds discuss other people, good minds discuss events, great minds discuss ideas". [10]

Maid

We need to respect our maids as well as we can, because let's be honest, they work for you just because they need money. And just because they need money, it doesn't mean you get to control them.

Everyone knows that it is a job but no one treats it as a job right? Let's say you work for a company, and your boss is pressuring you in many ways and controlling major aspects of your life. Now, what does that result in? It affects your mental health and your productivity. You will start hating your boss.

Now, what's the difference between you. The injustice he did to you, you are the repeating the nasty process by doing the same thing to your maid which isn't healthy for neither of you.

Slavery ended a long time ago but still, people are abusing their maids physically and mentally. Just because you have the power of hierarchy and money, it doesn't mean you can abuse them. Don't treat them like slaves, because they aren't. And if you really believe that they are your slaves, then almost everyone that works for someone is also considered to be a slave.

Respect maids, be kind to them, treat them like one of your family members. Treat them like you would want to be treated by your employer. Don't order them around. Request them politely. Give them time for rest and don't overwork them.

Sympathize with them. Help them out with the food they need, and appreciate them because what they're doing for a living is hard on mental and physical health.

Revenge

If someone hurts you, get away from them. Don't try to get revenge. Revenge won't heal your pain. Anything you do will come after you, whether bad or good.

So, be careful because when you are the least aware, consequences of your actions will come for you if not in this life, in the afterlife.

Values

Nothing would have value in life if the opposite of it didn't exist, for example, if there weren't evil there wouldn't be good.

We shouldn't get our value from materials, we give materials value.

We shouldn't get our value from people's tongues, you value yourself.

Entertainment

There are a lot of ways we can entertain ourselves with, such as movies and video games. But what I find people do for entertainment is literally eat, watch or play and then sleep. That's it.

Wasting your time like that is such a mistake. Most young people's lifestyle actually includes these for entertainment. As they believe they are young, and believe they just have to care about the present, it seems like they forgot about the future.

I get that, the way entertainment creators market their products is so attractive, but you need to control yourself from playing and watching all the time. If not, you're going to face a lot of problems in the future.

You shouldn't play when you have things to do. When you finish every task that you have to do, reward yourself with some entertainment but don't let it distract you from being productive. Keep things responsible and reasonable. Don't let it control you, you should be in charge of yourself.

As for games, I believe you should minimize it as much as you could. Games are so bad for our health that you would be shocked to know. The more we love it, the more we are passionate about it. More is the passion, the more anger it creates, which in the first place contravene with why we do it in the first place, for entertainment and relaxation.

All of that being said, we need to keep in mind that entertainment is the easiest and most common way to spread chaos. So, be careful.

Home

If your home is on fire, you'll feel like the whole world on fire. It will legitimately feel like the end of the world for you.

There's a strong meaning behind the word 'home'. It can be just a physical meaning, like its value being just that of the property's, no attachments present. It can be non-physical too, just like your inner self.

But in general, the idea of home is a place where you can feel safe, where you have privacy and it's where your real identity lies. It's your what they call a 'safe space'. If it gets corrupted, you'll get corrupted too. If you don't feel comfortable in your shell, you can't feel comfortable anywhere.

Build your home and then face the world.

Humor

Having a sense of humor is crucial because it can help with our mental and physical health, make us forget the hard times and see the bright side of life.
Humor is one of human's best surviving tools.

Curiosity

Curiosity is important to have because it keeps our minds active, but don't let your curiosity turn into nosiness in people's affairs.
Mind your own business.

Discipline

Discipline helps people to build a reliable personality, which will definitely lead to your success. Discipline helps you with time management, makes you more reliable, gives you the ability to manage emotions and kills the probability of unnecessary problems cropping up due to lack of discipline.

So set your priorities. Discipline your actions, mind and heart because discipline is the bridge that straightly leads you to your goals and accomplishments.

Change

Many people want change in same place or part of their life. Some people fail and give up. The secret to positive change is never giving up.

Divide your aim of life into smaller goals. Achieve them gradually. It would make them much easier and achievable. We must understand that every change demands sacrifices and a strong will without which, no dynamic, life-changing events would come. So, you should sacrifice what you have for what you need.

Everything is a cycle, demanding for change before time is demanding to change that cycle. Remember that, peace is all about the middle zone. Change on the other hand, lies on either side of peace. You don't have to have balance in everything. With balance you'll always be in your comfort zone and change will never come to you.

Without change, the same mistakes are to be done over and over again throughout generations.

In the end

Everything in life has positive and negative aspects. We can't control all of them most of the time and that's a fact. But doing what is right despite the positive and negative aspects and feelings is a choice.

To know what's right, we should take perspective of people around us into consideration. But at the end, religion should be the main decider at the end and that's my recipe for a better life. As easy as it may sound, it is as hard as people think it is.

Live your life the way you want. Enjoy it. Value yourself well in your own way. Try doing the right things and seek the truth. See the beauty of the world. Learn to take responsibility as an individual.

Together we can make the world a better place.

My intentions in writing this book was to share my thoughts and discuss things that you might use or experience in your life. And maybe I can help you change your thinking for the better. It's our thoughts that make us who we really are.

I am happy and grateful for sharing this with the world. Even if it only helps a single person, I'd still consider it as a win. Lastly, I want to thank everyone that has helped me in any way possible; friends, family and all the wise men that I quoted.

That is the philosophy of my life, what about yours?

References

[1] P. Junja, "MSG Management Study   Guide," Different Types of Power, 2015. [Online]. Available: https://www.managementstudyguide.com/types-of-power.htm. [Accessed: 23-Nov-2021].

[2] Chris drew, "The 4 types of critical thinking skills - explained! (2021)," Helpful Professor, 23-Nov-2019. [Online]. Available: https://helpfulprofessor.com/thinking-skills/ . [Accessed: 23-Nov-2021].

[3] John 8:32 then you will know the truth, and the truth will set you free.". [Online]. Available: https://biblehub.com/john/8-32.htm. [Accessed: 23-Nov-2021].

[4] T. Williams, "Steve Harvey slammed for claiming men and women can't be friends in resurfaced clip," Capital XTRA, 28-Apr-2021. [Online]. Available: https://www.capitalxtra.com/news/steve-harvey-men-

women-cant-be-friends-backlash-video/. [Accessed: 23-Nov-2021].

[5] "The Holy Quran, Chapter 9, verse 51," Islamic Sharing RSS. [Online]. Available: https://islamicsharing.com/quran/the-holy-quran-chapter-9-verse-51.html. [Accessed: 23-Nov-2021].

[6] J. Peterson, "Jordan B. Peterson quote: 'if you are not willing to be a fool, you can't become a master.",'" Quotefancy. [Online]. Available: https://quotefancy.com/quote/2564260/Jordan-B-Peterson-If-you-are-not-willing-to-be-a-fool-you-can-t-become-a-master. [Accessed: 23-Nov-2021].

[7] "Overt and covert human behavior," study and exam. [Online]. Available: https://www.studyandexam.com/overt-covert-behavior.html. [Accessed: 23-Nov-2021].

[8] D. Seland, Ed., "With great power comes great responsibility." Quality Magazine R33, 05-Apr-2018. [Online]. Available: https://www.qualitymag.com/articles/94643-with-

great-power-comes-great-responsibility. [Accessed: 23-Nov-2021].

[9] L. Shaffer, "'rich dad poor dad' author: Why millennials shouldn't save," CNBC, 24-Nov-2015. [Online]. Available: https://www.cnbc.com/2015/11/23/rich-dad-poor-dad-author-why-millennials-shouldnt-save.html. [Accessed: 23-Nov-2021].

[10] "Great minds discuss ideas. average minds discuss events. small minds discuss people.," Personal Excellence, 03-Apr-2021. [Online]. Available: https://personalexcellence.co/blog/great-minds/. [Accessed: 23-Nov-2021].

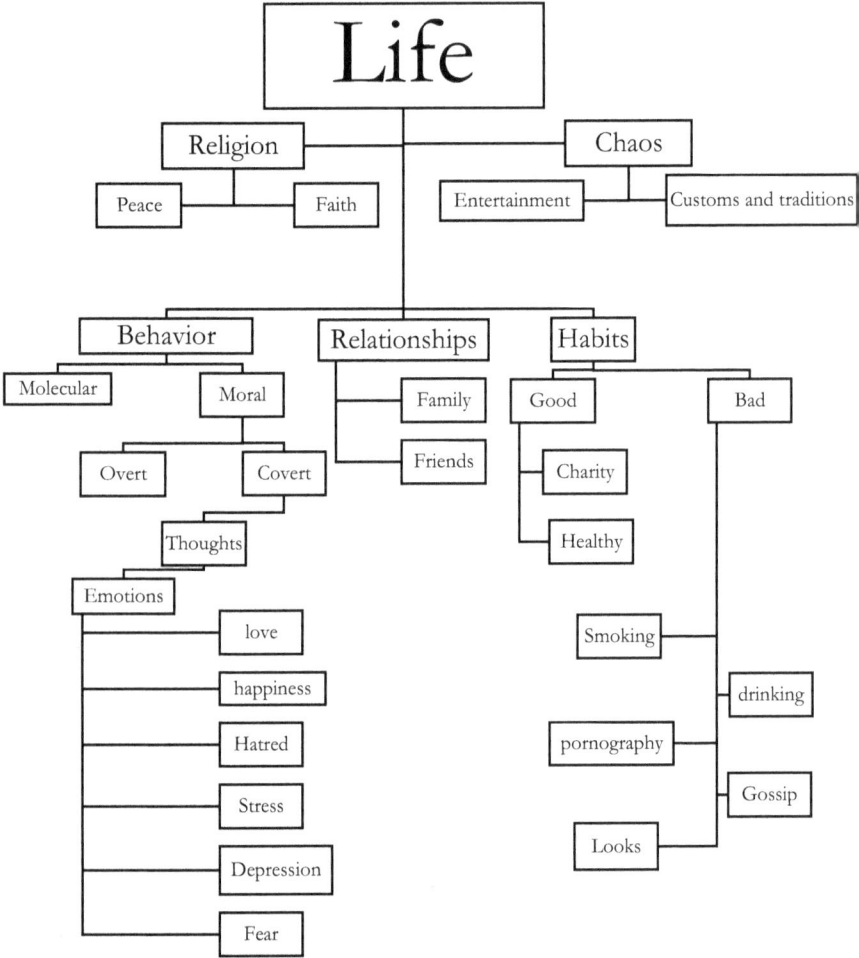

Life

Religion
- Peace
- Faith

Chaos
- Entertainment
- Customs and traditions

Behavior
- Molecular
- Moral
  - Overt
  - Covert
    - Thoughts
    - Emotions
      - love
      - happiness
      - Hatred
      - Stress
      - Depression
      - Fear

Relationships
- Family
- Friends

Habits
- Good
  - Charity
  - Healthy
- Bad
  - Smoking
  - drinking
  - pornography
  - Gossip
  - Looks

www.ingramcontent.com/pod-product-compliance
Lightning Source LLC
Chambersburg PA
CBHW071904020426
42331CB00010B/2659